Read & Respor

C000091614

Ages
7–11

Read & Respond

Ages
7–11

Author: Sarah Snashall and Huw Thomas

Commissioning Editor: Rachel Mackinnon

Editor: Tracy Kewley

Assistant Editor: Niamh O'Carroll

Series Designer: Anna Oliwa

Designer: Liz Gilbert

Illustrations: Charles Keeping and Sarah Warburton

Text © 2010 Sarah Snashall and Huw Thomas © 2010 Scholastic Ltd

Designed using Adobe InDesign

Published by Scholastic Ltd,
Book End, Range Road, Witney,
Oxfordshire OX29 0YD
www.scholastic.co.uk

Printed by Bell & Bain
2 3 4 5 6 7 8 9   2 3 4 5 6 7 8 9

British Library Cataloguing-in-Publication Data
A catalogue record for this book is available from
the British Library.
ISBN 978-1407-11898-7

Acknowledgements

The publishers gratefully acknowledge permission to reproduce the following copyright material: **B L Kearley Ltd** for the use of illustrations from *The Highwayman* by Alfred Noyes illustrated by Charles Keeping, illustrations © 1981 Charles Keeping (1981 Oxford University Press). **Oxford University Press** for the use of the cover of *The Highwayman* by Alfred Noyes, illustrated by Charles Keeping. **The Society of Authors** as the literary representatives of the Estate of Alfred Noyes for the use of text extracts from *The Highwayman* by Alfred Noyes © 1913, renewed 1941, Alfred Noyes (1981 Oxford University Press).

Every effort has been made to trace copyright holders for the works reproduced in this book, and the publishers apologise for any inadvertent omissions.

The Highwayman

About the poem

The Highwayman was published in 1907 but is set around 100 years earlier in a time when highwaymen were common. (King George is mentioned in the poem and there was a King George on the throne from 1714 to 1830.) The figure of the highwayman was greatly romanticised, both in ballads of the time and in literature of the 20th century. Referred to as 'gentlemen of the road', they were regarded as high-born and gallant; it was believed that they never robbed from women and that they only targeted the rich.

The Highwayman has been popular ever since its publication due to the tragedy of the romance, the melodrama of the story and the power of the verse. The emotion of the story rests on the doomed nature of the relationship – a highwayman is fated to be caught. Even in death, Bess and the highwayman cannot be together. The lovers are put in stark contrast against the soldiers and Tim, and their bravery and love are seen as transcendent emotions against the drunkenness and lewdness of the soldiers and the bitterness of Tim. The poetry itself is simple, but effective, with rhythmic repetition of lines, clever use of the colour red, references to the moon and changes in pace.

Illustrator Charles Keeping's evocative style is a perfect companion to *The Highwayman*. He is particularly enthusiastic at illustrating horror and the grotesque (as his illustrations for *Beowulf* also demonstrate) and some of his most successful illustrations for *The Highwayman* are those of Tim and the soldiers, and of the highwayman's face when he hears that Bess has died.

This is a great book to use in upper Key Stage 2. It can be used for understanding poetic techniques but the story can be used for studying narrative to great effect. Higher order comprehension skills and critical faculties can be developed by bringing out the difference between what the reader knows and feels and what the characters know and feel. Much of the emotion the reader feels comes from this; the reader is powerless to stop the inevitable happening and sees the futility of Bess' death at the end.

About the author

Alfred Noyes was born in Wolverhampton in 1880. He grew up in Wales and went to Oxford University, though he didn't get a degree. He spent much of his life in the United States and Canada but came back to Britain during the First World War and wrote propaganda material. His first collection of poems, *The Loom of Years*, was published in 1902. *The Highwayman* was published in 1907 as part of a collection called *Forty Singing Seamen and Other Poems*. He wrote poetry and later religious commentary for the rest of his life. He died in 1958.

About the illustrator

Charles Keeping (1924–1988) was a major illustrator in the 1970s. He illustrated editions of *Beowulf* and *The Lady of Shalot*, and the works of Leon Garfield and Rosemary Sutcliffe. He won many awards including The Kate Greenaway Medal twice and the Carnegie Medal.

Facts and figures
Since its first publication in 1907, *The Highwayman* has been published in numerous different forms, including many poetry collections and MP3 downloads. This illustrated edition was first published in 1981 and has sold 270,000 copies in the UK. Charles Keeping won The Kate Greenaway Medal in 1981 for his illustrations for the poem.

Guided reading

Introducing the book

Look together at the image on the cover. What type of story do the children think it might be? Look at the way the image is drawn with white on black. What does this suggest to the children about the story? (Possibly that it's an old or mysterious story.) Take note of the children's answers to check after the first reading of the poem.

Place the poem in its historical context. Tell the children that this is a narrative poem, set in the 18th or 19th century (but written at the beginning of the 20th century). Talk about the character on the horse and define the word 'highwayman' (a man who stops people travelling at night and robs them – basically a mugger). Explain that, in Victorian literature, the highwayman was often portrayed as romantic and exciting: handsome, masked and elegantly dressed. Explain that a highwayman would always be secretive and at risk of being captured.

The highwayman came riding

Read the first two pages aloud, with drama and expression. Talk about the rhyme scheme (a, a, b, c, c, b) and the effect of the repeated words in lines 4 and 5 (adds drama). Explain that this repetition is a feature throughout the poem. Ask the children to take turns reading verses aloud to become familiar with them. Enjoy the language of the first stanza and discuss the effectiveness of the similes *torrent of darkness*, *ghostly galleon tossed upon cloudy seas* and *ribbon of moonlight*.

Ask: *What does the description of the highwayman evoke?* (He is portrayed as an attractive figure, and Charles Keeping has drawn him as such, though perhaps more successfully in the fourth illustration of the character than the second. He is richly, fashionably and neatly dressed, and well-armed. He is attractive and dangerous.)

Read the text on the second spread. What do the children think might happen next in the story? Ask: *What might be the problem of a young girl loving a highwayman?*

One kiss, my bonny sweetheart

Read the poem from the beginning again to the page that ends *and galloped away to the west.* Focus on the character of Tim. Gather children's responses to the description and image of Tim. Charles Keeping has drawn Tim almost as a monster.

Ask for predictions about Tim's importance to the plot. Note the fact that when we look at the highwayman through Tim's eyes, he becomes a *robber* rather than the romantic *highwayman*. Talk about the drama of the situation: a silent inn, the young girl meeting a wanted man and the mad man listening in the darkness.

Turn to the page beginning *'One kiss my bonny sweetheart…'.* Here the repeated lines are about watching by moonlight – what effect does that have? (Romance and mystery perhaps?) Ask: *Why would people watch by night and not by day?* Draw out the evocation of secrecy and also remind the children of the thoughts they had about the cover. Ask: *Does moonlight connect with this ghostly image?*

Read the next page (beginning *He rose upright in the stirrups*) again and get over the 'yuck' factor regarding romance. Note: he does not kiss her – why not? (It's probably best to avoid the word 'erotic'!)

A red-coat troop came marching

Focus on the next two pages, showing Bess' view from the casement window. What is the effect of suddenly having only one line per page? (It slows down the pace as Bess waits.) Unpick the fact that Bess is waiting for the highwayman and that it is her view of the empty road that Charles Keeping has shown. Note the passage of time through the changing shading in these images and the one on the next page, and the effect of the third image showing soldiers where Bess was expecting to see her highwayman.

Explain the role of the soldiers here. At this time – and the reference to King George dates the events somewhere in the reign of George III or George IV – the soldiers took on the

Guided reading

role that the police have today. How are the soldiers portrayed? (Rude and cruel through the text; mean and laughing through the images.) Compare the faces of the soldiers here with those of the highwayman on his horse and Bess at the casement.

Talk about the behaviour of the soldiers and how their treatment of Bess revolts us. Bess would have been terrified – tied up and kissed by drunk, *sniggering* soldiers. How precarious is her situation? What might happen to her?

Do the children think that the highwayman is going to be caught? Point out the lines *There was death at every window* and *She heard the dead man say*. What do these lines suggest? (That everyone in the inn believes he will be caught and killed.) Do the children think he should be caught?

Talk about the character of Bess. What do the children think she is like? What might her life be like? (Possibly boring and lonely.) What does she hope for? (Possibly some excitement.) What makes her happy?

Look at the stanza that starts *She twisted her hands behind her*. What is she trying to do? Make connections with action films where a hero or heroine tries to do the same thing. Ask the children to try and imagine Bess, frightened and tied up and waiting for hours for the highwayman to come, knowing that he'll be shot when he does. Ask: *What can she do to help? What is the advantage of Bess being able to touch the trigger? Why does she not try and free the rest of her hands?* Look at the image showing the musket wedged underneath Bess' breast. Do the children understand what will happen if she pulls the trigger?

In the moonlight

Read from *He did not come in the dawning* to *throbbed to her love's refrain* again and recap thoughts before reading on to end of the poem. Look at the spread beginning *Tlot-tlot; tlot-tlot!* The pace changes with the sound *Tlot-tlot*; after all the waiting, the highwayman has arrived and is shown in the road – the sixth time we see this view from the window.

Review what happens in that central shocking scene where Bess pulls the trigger. Did the children expect this? Were they shocked? The image on the right-hand side of the spread is pretty horrible, as is the phrase *Shattered her breast*.

Think about the character of the highwayman and how he must have felt when he heard the news about Bess. Look at the image of his shocked face. Read the text from *He turned* to *with the bunch of lace at his throat* and talk about what the highwayman does. Think through each movement, asking the children what he does and what he is thinking and feeling at the time. The details of where the soldiers find him are not given. Can the children imagine what might have happened? (Does he return to the inn?) Note the effectiveness of the episode being hidden and inferred.

Read the text on the spread beginning *Back, he spurred like a madman* and point out how, just before he dies, his spurs glow *blood-red* in the sun and his velvet coat is *wine-red*, pre-empting the blood he lies in at the end of the stanza. Talk about the use of the colour red in the poem, where most things are either black or white. What other instances can the children find? (The ribbon in Bess' hair and her red lips, and the *red-coat troop*.)

What would the children pick as the most important turning point in the book thus far, from the start to this section? (The arrival of the soldiers, or the death of Bess, or the death of the highwayman?) Can the children justify their answer?

And still of a winter's night…

Read the whole poem as a dramatic reading. Discuss the ghostly ending. Did the children find it spooky? If not, ask them to imagine the sound of the eerie whistling of the ghostly highwayman and the creepy tapping on the shutters. The story could have ended with the death of the highwayman, but what is the effect of the ghost story ending? The whole story almost becomes a ghost story as it becomes an explanation of a haunting. And the repeated phrase in every

Guided reading

stanza seems to reflect the repeated meeting of the haunted pair. Ask the children: *Were there any hints in the first part of the poem that this might end as a ghost story?* Look at all the references to moonlight in the book and reflect on how it all builds to this ghostly idea. Point out how the moon is referred to as a *ghostly galleon* on two occasions and how this adds to the atmosphere.

Look at the effect that Charles Keeping has created by turning black to white and white to black in his illustrations for the end of the book.

Return to the predictions made in the first two sessions and compare them with what actually happened. Discuss the children's overall impression of the poem and ask the children to read out their favourite pages and lines.

Shared reading

Extract 1

● Discuss the description of Tim. Underline the similes *mouldy hay* and *dumb as a dog* which link Tim to his job as an ostler (a stable hand). What does the phrase *His face was white and peaked* suggest? (That he is shocked by something, or that he is generally unhealthy.) What might *His eyes were hollows of madness* mean? (Wide and staring, as in Keeping's portrayal of him.)

● Ask: *How does Tim feel about Bess?* The repeated lines almost suggest that he's obsessed with her. Ask the children to infer how Tim might therefore feel about the highwayman.

● Talk about what feelings Bess might have about Tim. (Sympathy? Indifference? Disgust?) What tension could result from these conflicting feelings?

● But what advantage does Tim have over the highwayman? (He can work secretly because he's overlooked; he can use the soldiers to eliminate his rival.)

Extract 2

● Ask the children to pick out the stages of Bess' actions (she twists her hands, she writhes her hands, she stretches and strains her fingers, she touches the trigger with the tip of one finger). Circle and number them. In how many ways do her hands move?

● Discuss with the children what Bess does in the second stanza of the extract. (Nothing – she just waits and feels her blood pumping round her body.) Ask: *What is the effect of this?* (Builds the tension; we wait with Bess for the highwayman's arrival.)

● Time is very important in the poem. Ask: *How long does this episode take? What is the significance of midnight?*

● Discuss the line *She would not risk their hearing*. Why not? Why not try and free her hands so that she can shoot without killing herself? Why not shoot now? What is she trying to do?

Extract 3

● Before reading Extract 3, remind the children of the promise the highwayman made to Bess.

● Discuss the fact that Bess works so hard to save his life yet he dies anyway. Do the children think he knew that he headed for his death?

● Look at the contrast in the second stanza between his brave stance with his sword and his sudden death.

● Circle all the references to blood and blood-coloured items in these two stanzas.

● Point out how he is *Down like a dog*. Compare this to Tim, who is described as *Dumb as a dog*. Are Tim and the highwayman equal now?

● Point out how Alfred Noyes quickly makes the comparison between how the highwayman appeared at the beginning *with a bunch of lace at his chin* and how he lies now with *the bunch of lace at his throat*. (The replacement of the word *chin* with *throat* fits the rhyme of the two stanzas but the word *throat* in the latter scene also has a more sinister, deathly feel.)

Extract 1

And dark in the dark old inn-yard a stable-wicket creaked

Where Tim the ostler listened. His face was white and
peaked.

His eyes were hollows of madness, his hair like mouldy hay,

But he loved the landlord's daughter,

The landlord's red-lipped daughter.

Dumb as a dog he listened, and he heard the robber say—

Text © 1913, renewed 1941, Alfred Noyes; illustration © 1981, Charles Keeping.

Extract 2

She twisted her hands behind her; but all the knots held good!

She writhed her hands till her fingers were wet with sweat or blood!

They stretched and strained in the darkness, and the hours crawled by
   like years,

Till, now, on the stroke of midnight,

   Cold, on the stroke of midnight,

The tip of one finger touched it! The trigger at least was hers!

The tip of one finger touched it. She strove no more for the rest.

Up, she stood up to attention, with the muzzle beneath her breast.

She would not risk their hearing; she would not strive again;

For the road lay bare in the moonlight;

   Blank and bare in the moonlight;

And the blood of her veins, in the moonlight, throbbed to her
   love's refrain.

Text © 1913, renewed 1941, Alfred Noyes.

Extract 3

He turned. He spurred to the west; he did not know who stood

Bowed, with her head o'er the musket, drenched with her
    own red blood!

Not till the dawn he heard it, and his face grew grey to hear

How Bess, the landlord's daughter,

    The landlord's black-eyed daughter,

Had watched for her love in the moonlight, and died in
    the darkness there.

Back, he spurred like a madman, shouting a curse to the sky,

With the white road smoking behind him and his rapier brandished high

Blood-red were his spurs i' the golden noon; wine-red was his
    velvet coat;

When they shot him down on the highway,

    Down like a dog on the highway,

And he lay in his blood on the highway, with the bunch of lace
    at his throat.

SCHOLASTIC
www.scholastic.co.uk

Plot, character and setting

Responding to characters

> **Objective:** To infer writers' perspectives from what is written and from what is implied.
> **What you need:** Copies of *The Highwayman*, photocopiable page 15.

What to do
● Ask the children to focus on the characters (the highwayman, Bess, Tim and the red-coats) as they listen to you read through the poem again.
● At the end of the reading, ask the children for their immediate thoughts about Bess. Note down their responses (they might say romantic, brave, beautiful, resourceful, foolish, controlled, true to her love). Can they explain these thoughts? Encourage them to find passages in the poem – those that describe Bess and those that describe her actions – that support their thoughts. Can the children find any additional evidence in the illustrations?
● As a class, create a couple of sentences about Bess in the children's own words, for example, 'Bess loves the highwayman more than she loves life'; 'Bess is so controlled and determined she's able to hide her plan from the soldiers'.
● Hand out copies of photocopiable page 15. Ask the children to describe in their own words their thoughts about each character and then to justify their thoughts by referring to events or passages from the poem.

> **Differentiation**
> **For older/more confident learners:** Challenge children to provide two separate thoughts about each character, each with a justification from the poem.
> **For younger/less confident learners:** Ask children to focus on just two characters.

Why?

> **Objective:** To understand underlying themes, causes and points of view.
> **What you need:** Copies of *The Highwayman*, photocopiable page 16.

What to do
● Explain to the children that they are going to explore the things that they are not told in the poem and see if they can infer the reasons behind some of the events.
● Ask: *Why did the soldiers come to the inn?* Discuss the first child's answer then challenge it with alternative thoughts. *Did they come because Tim summoned them? Were they searching for the highwayman anyway? Perhaps the landlord summoned them, worried about his daughter? Perhaps they were stationed in the area and just came for a drink?* Try to illustrate to the children that there is no way of knowing from the text, but encourage them to provide justification for their answer – Tim's actions are suspicious early on; the red-coats tie up Bess as soon as they've had a drink as if this was their plan.
● Organise the children into appropriate groups for group discussion. Provide each group with a copy of photocopiable page 16. Ask the children to talk about each question in their groups. Encourage the children to think as widely as possible about each question, coming up with as many possible answers as they can.
● Hand out individual copies of photocopiable page 16 and ask the children to fill in their own answers to these questions.

> **Differentiation**
> **For older/more confident learners:** Challenge these children to explain their thinking behind each answer.
> **For younger/less confident learners:** Ask these children to choose the two questions they find the most interesting.

Plot, character and setting

Between the lines

> **Objective:** To make notes on and use evidence from across a text to explain events or ideas.
> **What you need:** Copies of *The Highwayman*, photocopiable page 17.
> **Cross-curricular link:** History (linking events).

What to do

● This activity provides further work on inference. Read the stanza that starts *Back, he spurred like a madman.* Ask: *Where was the highwayman when the soldiers saw him?* Explain that we don't know because this scene is not described.

● Hand out individual copies of photocopiable page 17 and ask the children to cut out and sequence the events in the order in which they would have happened. (There is no way of knowing that Tim loved Bess before she met the highwayman, but one imagines that he did.)

● Once the children have re-sequenced the events, ask volunteers to explain how we can infer that these events took place. For example, we assume that Tim has called the red-coats because we know that he has overheard the lovers talking and that he is in love with Bess.

● Ask: *Are there any events on the sheet that might have happened differently?* We don't know that the landlord is not around to help his daughter; this is just one suggestion. We don't know whether it is Tim who tells the red-coats but we are lead to believe that it is. All the other events must happen for the story to follow the line it does.

> **Differentiation**
> **For older/more confident learners:** Challenge children to link the boxes from photocopiable page 17 with events described in the poem.
> **For younger/less confident learners:** Let children focus on ordering the events.

Straight and still

> **Objective:** To understand how writers use different structures to create coherence and impact.
> **What you need:** Copies of *The Highwayman*, photocopiable page 18.
> **Cross-curricular link:** PSHE.

What to do

● Explain to the children that you are going to be spending time focusing in on the key scene in the poem – Bess' death.

● Without reading the text first, hand out copies of photocopiable page 18. Ask the children to cut up the boxes and put them in the correct order.

● Ask the children to check the order they have chosen against the text in the book and re-order the boxes if necessary. Did they find they needed to re-order the text at all? Perhaps they misplaced *She heard the dead man*, as this comes earlier in the passage than they might have remembered.

● Spend time ensuring that the children have understood each line. Talk about the use of the phrase *dead man* here. The highwayman is not dead at this point so why does Bess refer to him in this way? (Because he will be if he arrives while the redcoats are there? Because the redcoats will not rest until he is dead?)

> **Differentiation**
> **For older/more confident learners:** Challenge children to take each box and talk about how each event leads to the next.
> **For younger/less confident learners:** Ask children to find each bit of text in the poem.

Plot, character and setting

Questions, questions

> **Objective:** To make notes on and use evidence from across a text to explain events or ideas.
> **What you need:** Copies of *The Highwayman*.
> **Cross-curricular links:** Philosophy, thinking skills.

What to do

● Ask the children to work in pairs to draw up a list of questions that could be asked to another pair about the poem. Suggest use of starters such as 'Why…' or 'What will happen when…'. In this way the children will develop their skills by rehearsing in their own heads the comprehension process of asking questions, anticipating answers and then finding out what happens. Encourage the children to ask questions about what characters will do, why they will do it and what outcomes will occur.

● As a class, gather together a list of the most interesting questions and discuss how these questions show us how we think as readers – wondering when characters first meet, what will happen to them in the future and so on.

● Talk about how good writers make us wonder in this way as we read.

> **Differentiation**
> **For older/more confident learners:** Challenge children to rank questions by most to least interesting.
> **For younger/less confident learners:** Encourage children to ask their own questions as readers.

The gunshot

> **Objective:** To infer writers' perspectives from what is written and from what is implied.
> **What you need:** Copies of *The Highwayman*.
> **Cross-curricular links:** Drama, PSHE.

What to do

● Ask the children to imagine hearing the gunshot from the perspective of the different characters: the landlord, the soldiers, Tim and the highwayman. We know how the highwayman reacts when he hears the shot, but what does he think and what does he know? How would the soldiers have reacted? Note that this was not part of the plan. What about the landlord and Tim?

● Organise the children to work in small groups of about three or four. Ask them to take each character in turn and to discuss the different reactions the characters will have, making notes of their thoughts. Who does each character think has been shot, if anyone? What does each character do? Ensure that each group has a copy of the text and encourage them to refer to it for details.

● After the children have finished their discussion, capture the different groups' thoughts on a class spidergram, with the word 'gunshot' at the centre and the characters' names around the outside. What variety of feelings and reactions have the groups come up with?

● Probe the children's thinking deeper. Might the soldiers worry about what their superiors might say when they find out what's happened? Imagine the landlord entering his daughter's bedroom and seeing the scene before him. How will Tim feel when he finds out that he has caused Bess' death?

> **Differentiation**
> **For older/more confident learners:** Challenge children to imagine that different soldiers had different feelings – what might these be? Ask them to imagine an argument that might take place between them as they look for someone to blame.
> **For younger/less confident learners:** Ask children to focus on just two characters – perhaps Tim and one of the soldiers.

Plot, character and setting

Highwayman feelings

Objective: To explore how writers use language for comic and dramatic effects.
What you need: Copies of *The Highwayman*, sticky notes.
Cross-curricular link: PSHE.

What to do
● Read aloud the first three stanzas and ask for suggestions about how the highwayman and Bess might feel at this stage of the story. For example, we assume that the highwayman is happy at the beginning, half suggested by the fact that everything about him twinkles.
● Organise the children into groups of three or four and give each group a copy of the text and some sticky notes. Ask the children to go through the poem and to stick notes on each page describing what the characters are feeling at that point. If possible, they should quote the phrase from the poem that links to this feeling. For example: 'Bess is in love. She is *plaiting a love-knot* in her hair.' Remind them that characters will have different feelings at other points in the story, and that other characters will have different feelings.
● Once they've been through the poem once, ask the children to look for points in the story where different characters feel different things, for example when the highwayman and Bess first meet, Bess and Tim feel differently; when the soldiers come, Bess and the soldiers feel differently.
● At the end of the session, gather the sticky notes from each group on a large sheet of paper for display.

Differentiation
For older/more confident learners: Challenge children to discuss how our reactions differ from those of the characters.
For younger/less confident learners: Set children the task of reading and recording the variety of feelings without needing to refer back to the text.

Focus on

Objective: To explore how writers use language for comic and dramatic effects.
What you need: Copies of *The Highwayman*.
Cross-curricular link: PSHE.

What to do
● Ask the children to work in pairs and to choose two pages from the book to concentrate on.
● Ask the children to read the pages together to become experts on the content, mysteries and importance of the pages. Can they explain why this episode is integral to the story? What do they think are the most important bits of language in their extract? Ask them to discuss in their pairs what is said in these lines and also what is unsaid. What do we infer, what would we imagine if we pictured this section in our minds?
● Ask them to focus on creating a dramatic reading of their passage – how do they think those important lines should be read? Can they practise getting the right expression and tone for their reading? Encourage them to read aloud to each other, commenting on each other's reading.
● If appropriate, ask the children to learn their verses by heart.

Differentiation
For older/more confident learners: Challenge children to extend their focus to the pages on either side.
For younger/less confident learners: Give children a set of four lines or one page. Ask them to concentrate on understanding the content.

Plot, character and setting

Responding to characters

● Record how you feel about the characters in *The Highwayman* and why.

What we feel:

And why:

What we feel:

And why:

What we feel:

And why:

What we feel:

And why:

Illustrations © 1981, Charles Keeping.

Plot, character and setting

Why?

● We are left to infer many of the characters' actions in *The Highwayman*. Why do you think the following things happened?

Why did the red-coats come to the inn?

Why did they tie Bess up?

Why did Bess pull the trigger?

Why did the highwayman 'turn and spur'?

Why did the highwayman come back?

Why does the highwayman's ghost return?

Plot, character and setting

Between the lines

● The following events are not in the poem but we can infer that they may have happened. Cut out the statements and arrange them in the order in which they may have occurred.

Someone tells the highwayman about Bess' death.
Tim falls in love with Bess.
The red-coats see the highwayman approaching.
Bess first meets the highwayman.
Bess serves ale to the red-coats.
Tim tells the red-coats about Bess' planned meeting with the highwayman.
The landlord goes away.
Someone sees the ghost of Bess and the highwayman.

Plot, character and setting

SECTION 4

Straight and still

● Cut out these lines from *The Highwayman* and arrange them in the correct order. Check your order against the poem.

She drew one last deep breath.
She strove no more for the rest.
She twisted her hands behind her.
She heard the dead man.
Drenched with her own red blood!
Warned him – with her death.
She stood up, straight and still.
The trigger at least was hers!

www.scholastic.co.uk

Talk about it

Responding to the images

Objective: To use a range of oral techniques to present persuasive arguments and engaging narratives.
What you need: Copies of *The Highwayman*, A3 paper.
Cross-curricular link: Art and design.

What to do

● Look together at the illustration of Tim the ostler. Ask the children for their thoughts about the illustration, for example, mad-looking, scary, unattractive. What do the children think about the way he is holding his hands?

● Arrange the children in discussion groups. Give each group a copy of *The Highwayman* and four sheets of A3 paper. Ask each group to agree on four illustrations to focus on. They should then work together to fill the paper with thoughts about the illustrations one by one. Remind them to capture everyone's thoughts and to ensure that everyone has a chance to talk.

● Once the groups have finished, ask them to talk further with their group about how the illustration enhances their enjoyment of the text. Can they admire the illustrator's skill at portraying facial expressions? What do they think about Charles Keeping's repeated use of the view from the window?

Differentiation
For older/more confident learners: Challenge some children to compose some questions that they would like to ask Charles Keeping regarding the illustrations. How do they think he might answer? (The illustrator died in 1988.)
For younger/less confident learners: Younger groups of children might like to work together to put the images in order. This in itself should generate discussion.

Lines

Objective: To use and explore different question types and different ways words are used, including in formal and informal contexts.
What you need: Copies of *The Highwayman*, photocopiable page 22.

What to do

● Ask the children to work in their groups. Give each group a copy of photocopiable page 22 and ask them to cut out the six lines from the poem and to place them face down on the table between them.

● Tell them to turn over one of the lines and discuss as a group what they think it means, why Alfred Noyes phrased it the way he did and what emotions the lines evoke in them. For example, for *I'll come to thee by moonlight, though hell should bar the way,* the children might talk about how, when you read this line the first time, it sounds as if the highwayman is just talking expansively for effect, but on a second reading we pick up on the clue about moonlight and his promise to return even if he's dead. He keeps his promise and this line has added significance at the end of the poem when the highwayman's ghost comes riding. This might make them feel chilled on a second reading.

● Which are the children's favourite lines? Challenge them to agree a group ranking for the lines.

Differentiation
For older/more confident learners: Challenge children to write a paragraph about their favourite line, capturing the group's thoughts.
For younger/less confident learners: Locating the lines in the text might be an appropriate activity.

Talk about it

Who thinks there?

Objective: To understand underlying themes, causes and points of view.
What you need: Copies of *The Highwayman*, a copy of photocopiable page 23 for each pair of children.
Cross-curricular link: PSHE.

What to do
● Explain to the children that they will be working with a partner to talk about the characters' feelings at specific points in the poem. Hand out a copy of photocopiable page 23 to each pair of children and ensure that they also have a copy of the text.
● Ask the children to look at the first thought bubble: 'I'm so jealous'. Can they work out with their talk partner whose thought this could be and at what stage in the poem the thought may have occurred? Agree as a class that it is Tim's thought,

as he overhears Bess and the highwayman talk. Ask the children to record their ideas in the space and then to discuss and record their ideas about why he feels this. Encourage the children to refer to the text and illustrations as they talk. Agree that Tim is in love with Bess himself.
● Give the children time to talk and fill in the rest of the sheet. Point out that the second thought could be one of two people (Bess or the highwayman at the beginning).

Differentiation
For older/more confident learners: Challenge children to set new thought clues for their classmates.
For younger/less confident learners: For some children it will be enough just to locate the thought in the poem.

Telling our story

Objective: To use a range of oral techniques to present persuasive arguments and engaging narratives.
What you need: Copies of *The Highwayman*.
Cross-curricular links: PSHE, drama.

What to do
● Ask each group to take one of the following episodes and to allocate the characters between them. You might want to make the groups of unequal size as any number of children could be the soldiers, all of whom could have a different reaction to the events (for example, horror, fear, guilt, callous indifference).
　● The meeting between Bess and the highwayman. Characters: Bess, Tim, the highwayman.
　● The episode where Bess is tied up. Characters: Bess, the soldiers, the landlord and Tim.

　● Bess' death. Characters: Bess, the soldiers, the landlord, Tim, the highwayman.
　● The end. Characters: Bess' ghost, the highwayman's ghost, the landlord, Tim, an inn guest who see the ghosts.
● Ask the groups to talk in character about the event as if they were remembering it a few years later, for example: 'I was so excited when the highwayman visited me – my life at the inn was boring and hard work and he was so glamorous'; 'I was so jealous when I saw Bess and the highwayman – I had to think of a way to get rid of him'; 'When I saw that she'd shot herself I felt sick'.

Differentiation
For older/more confident learners: Improvise a conversation between two characters years later.
For younger/less confident learners: Join a group of children taking on the role of the soldiers.

Talk about it

Read aloud

Objective: To perform a scripted scene making use of dramatic conventions.
What you need: Copies of *The Highwayman*.
Cross-curricular link: Drama.

What to do
● *The Highwayman* is made to be read aloud. Work together to create a class performance of the poem.
● Divide up the poem among the groups in the class. This could be done by page or stanza, or even better by character. Allocate the verses that are mainly focused on the highwayman to one group, Bess to another, Tim to another and the red-coats to the final group.
● Encourage each group to discuss how their verses could be read, for example snarling, screaming or in a spooky voice. Invite them to talk about what feelings each verse creates in the listener, for example fear or shock, and how they can capture this in their voice as they read the poem aloud.
● Ask each group to divide up the lines they have between them and then to learn them by heart.
● After the children have had enough time to practise, create your class performance.

Differentiation
For older/more confident learners: Challenge children to act out the drama as they learn their lines, putting emotion into lines that depict the character's focus.
For younger/less confident learners: Provide children with a chosen set of lines with a chosen emotion tagged to them.

Mysteries

Objective: To present a spoken argument, sequencing points logically, defending views with evidence and making use of persuasive language.
What you need: Copies of *The Highwayman*, photocopiable page 24.
Cross-curricular link: PSHE.

What to do
● Talk to the class about the role of mystery in this poem. Much of the tension comes from the fact that the reader knows things that the characters do not.
● Give each pair of children photocopiable page 24 and ask them to consider the statements on the sheet. Do they agree with all of the statements?
● Can the children find further examples of things that the reader knows but the characters do not (including things that can be inferred)?
● As a class, work through the examples on the sheet and the children's examples, inviting opinions about each of the statements. Some of the points are questionable, which should lead to lively debate. For example, 'We know that Bess and the highwayman have met but the landlord does not'. Do the children think the landlord really is unaware of the relationship between his daughter and the highwayman, or is he just turning a blind eye? Is it possible that he informed the red-coats that the highwayman would be coming to the inn? Why might he do this?

Differentiation
For older/more confident learners: Challenge children to create a list of what we don't know: where the landlord is, where the soldiers meet the highwayman, what happens to Tim and so on.
For younger/less confident learners: Ask children to focus on the illustrations and to decide what the characters know and don't know at each of these points.

Lines

● Cut out the following lines from *The Highwayman* and arrange them face down on the table. Turn over one of the lines and discuss it as a group. Repeat with four other lines.

I'll come to thee by moonlight, though hell should bar the way.

There was death at every window.

She heard the dead man say – look for me by moonlight.

The trigger at least was hers!

And the blood of her veins, in the moonlight, throbbed to her love's refrain.

Back, he spurred like a madman, shouting a curse to the sky.

SCHOLASTIC
www.scholastic.co.uk

Talk about it

Who thinks there?

● Discuss these thoughts with your partner. For each one, agree together whose thought it could be and when and why they thought it. Some of the thoughts could belong to different characters.

I'm so jealous.

When? _____

Why? _____

Who? _____

_____

When? _____

Why? _____

_____

I'm so happy!

Who? _____

What are they doing here?

When? _____

Why? _____

Who? _____

_____

When? _____

Why? _____

_____

I must save him!

Who? _____

What have they done to her?

When? _____

Why? _____

Who? _____

_____

■SCHOLASTIC
www.scholastic.co.uk

Mysteries

● Mystery plays an important role in *The Highwayman*. Much of the tension comes from the fact that the reader knows things that the characters do not. Discuss the statements below with a partner and decide if you think each one is true.

● Look through the book to see if you can find other examples of things that the reader knows but the characters do not and add these to the list.

We know...	when...
We know that Bess and the highwayman have met	when the landlord does not.
We know that the soldiers have come to the inn	when the highwayman does not.
We know that Bess has died	when the highwayman does not.

READ & RESPOND: Activities based on The Highwayman

Get writing

On the way

> **Objective:** To experiment with different narrative form and styles to write their own stories.
> **What you need:** Copies of *The Highwayman*, photocopiable page 28, writing materials.
> **Cross-curricular links:** Geography, art and design.

What to do

● Hand out a copy of photocopiable page 28 to each child. Explain that the sheet provides a frame for them to plan a journey that one of the characters in *The Highwayman* takes.
● Invite the children to work in pairs and to choose a character each to focus on. The cards on the photocopiable sheet should be cut out and placed face down on the table. The children can then take turns to choose a card and, together, come up with as many suggestions as they can for each of their characters' journeys.

● Point out that there could be a good reason for a character being chased (for example, someone could be chasing Bess with a message from her father or the highwayman).
● Once the children have discussed their ideas in pairs, ask them to choose six areas to focus on individually and to plan out their story. They could stick their cards down in the correct order for their story, and make notes around them.
● Invite the children to write up their stories.

> **Differentiation**
> **For older/more confident learners:** Children could draw a map to accompany their stories.
> **For younger/less confident learners:** It might be enough for some children to fill in only four boxes and tell a story aloud about the journey.

Tim's story

> **Objective:** To understand underlying themes, causes and points of view.
> **What you need:** Copies of *The Highwayman*, photocopiable page 29, writing materials.
> **Cross-curricular link:** PSHE.

What to do

● Tell the children that they are going to focus on how Tim feels about the events of the story by writing his diary entry for four points in the story. Remind the children about the work they've done on inferring the events not described in the poem.
● Hand out copies of photocopiable page 29. Discuss together the various points in the story. They can use material from the poem for inspiration for the first entry but explain that

they have a free rein for the other entries, as these are events that we can only infer.
● Talk about diary-writing styles. Explain that in many cases writers just write in note form, and encourage the children to write in this way, for example 'Overheard Bess talking to the robber. Gutted. How can I get rid of him?' A fuller entry could be written later if appropriate.

> **Differentiation**
> **For older/more confident learners:** Challenge children to write a diary entry for Tim after he has had an encounter with the ghosts.
> **For younger/less confident learners:** Ask children to focus on writing an entry for the night he overheard Bess and the highwayman meet, as this can be based on the poem itself.

Get writing

Haunting

Objective: To explore how writers use language for comic and dramatic effects.
What you need: Photocopiable page 30, writing materials.

What to do
● If the children in your class are not too sensitive, encourage them to write their own ghost story. They can create a ghost or a strange apparition (it doesn't need to be evil or scary).
● Hand out copies of photocopiable page 30 which provides them with prompts to structure their story planning. Talk together about their options. Will their creature be good or evil? Will it be sad or funny? Explain that the atmosphere of their final story will depend on the details they create for their ghost.
● Look together at the last box. The poem of *The*

Highwayman is basically the 'back story' for the ghost story. Encourage the children to develop their thoughts on their ghost's 'back story' as this will help them to give substance to their ghost. Perhaps their ghost was disappointed in love, or wronged in some way, or needs to tell someone something?
● Allow the children time to fill in their sheets and then to spend time talking about and revising their thoughts with a talk partner before finally planning and writing their ghost story.

Differentiation
For older/more confident learners: Encourage children to make links between objects and events in the past and to bring these into the ghost story.
For younger/less confident learners: Ask children to work together to create a shared story in a guided session.

Watch for me

Objective: To select words and language drawing on their knowledge of literary features and formal and informal writing.
What you need: Copies of *The Highwayman*, writing materials.

What to do
● Talk to the class about the phrase *Watch for me by moonlight*. It is such a poignant phrase in the context of the story. Find all the times it is repeated in the poem and talk about the effect of this. Look through the poem for other rhythmic refrains such as *He did not come...* What is the effect of these lines? Does it give the poem the atmosphere of a fable perhaps?
● Ask the children to suggest other stories with repeated phrases. They might suggest 'Then I'll huff and I'll puff...' or 'Fee-fi-fo-fum'. These

refrains give character and feeling to the tale and the children's task is going to be to create their own repeated phrases for a tale of their own.
● Give groups of children access to dictionaries, a thesaurus and vocabulary charts, and challenge them to devise some new story phrases.
● Gather together a list of all the phrases the children have come up with. Ask the children to write a short story using their own phrase or a preferred phrase from the class list.

Differentiation
For older/more confident learners: Encourage children to devise a story where the phrase or refrain is central to the story.
For younger/less confident learners: Ask children to take one of the phrases discussed and use it in a story.

Get writing

The inn

> **Objective:** To set their own challenges to extend achievement and experience in writing.
> **What you need:** Writing materials.
> **Cross-curricular link:** History.

What to do

● Set the scene for the class: it is 2020 and two people visit the inn where the events of *The Highwayman* took place.

● Ask for suggestions as to what might happen. Maybe they hear that the inn is haunted but don't believe the stories, but then are woken at night by the sound of hooves. What would happen?

● Discuss how the visitors find out the tale behind the highwayman. Perhaps the visitors meet a descendant of the king's men, or they find Tim's diary, or maybe Bess' ghost points to the road and so on.

● Do the children think that the ghosts will be laid to rest at the end? If so, how?

● With help from volunteers from the class, storyboard the class story.

● Ask the children to work in pairs to recreate the storyboard for their own version of the story, inserting new storyboard boxes at the beginning, middle and end of the story and changing any details that they would like to.

> **Differentiation**
> **For older/more confident learners:** Ask children to particularly focus on the tension that will happen before the haunting is resolved.
> **For younger/less confident learners:** Ask children to list the types of thing that could happen in a scary inn, thinking of noises they might hear and what they might see.

Playscript

> **Objective:** To perform a scripted scene making use of dramatic conventions.
> **What you need:** Copies of *The Highwayman*, writing materials.
> **Cross-curricular link:** Drama.

What to do

● Ask the children to work in groups of three and give each group a copy of *The Highwayman*. Ask them to look through the poem and together decide on a short scene or exchange that could have taken place in the course of the story, and to improvise it into a short scene. Tell them that once they have practised their scene, they will be asked to write it as a playscript. Potential exchanges could be between the highwayman, Bess and Tim; between two soldiers and Tim; or between Bess, a soldier and the landlord.

● Explain that you would like them to catch the tension in the scene. What is it about this scene that would make our hearts beat faster? How would they like the viewer to feel when watching the scene? Encourage them to end their scene on a cliffhanger.

● Once the threesomes have had a chance to practise their scene and perform it to another group, invite them to write their scene down as a playscript.

> **Differentiation**
> **For older/more confident learners:** Encourage children to include stage directions and director's annotations in their playscripts. Children could also be challenged to write a soliloquy for a character of their choice.
> **For younger/less confident learners:** Let children choose an illustration and imagine the exchange between the characters in it.

SECTION
6

On the way

● Plan a journey for a character of your choice from *The Highwayman*. Choose six of these elements to include in a story about their journey and write notes in the boxes.

A starting point	What they leave behind
Someone they meet along the way	An enemy
Someone who is chasing them	Someone who joins them on the journey
What they are looking for	The end of journey

Get writing

Tim's story

● Write some short diary entries for Tim the Ostler at different points in the poem.

What I felt about the highwayman and Bess:

How I ended up telling the king's men:

What I remember about the death of Bess:

What happened to me after these terrible days:

Illustration © 2010, Sarah Warburton.

Haunting

● Create your own ghost, monster or thing and use this sheet to plan a story for it.

What is it?
What does it say?
What does it want?
What do other people feel and say about it?
Why does it appear? What happened in the past?

Assessment

Assessment advice

The Highwayman is a wonderful piece of melodrama and, as such, it is a poem that aims to extract an emotional response from the reader. The book is an excellent vehicle for assessing children's abilities to verbalise feelings and emotions, both within the story, and how the reader responds to these feelings. When assessing the children's understanding of the poem we need to look for the following points:

● Do the children display an understanding of the characters and their point of view? Do the children understand what the characters are feeling at different points in the story?

● Do the children understand the emotional subtleties of the poem? Are they able to articulate how the emotions of the characters often conflict with the emotions of the reader and what the reader knows? It is this heightened, Level 5 type response that we really should tease out. (For example the lovers make us worry whether it will work out.)

● Are the children able to grasp the tension in the poem? Can they locate moments of tension and explain why they are tense?

● This is a relatively old poem. Can the children understand why the poem has enduring appeal? Can they talk about other stories that resemble it and what features about it make it one that stays in the memory?

Along the way

> **Assessment focuses:** To understand, describe, select or retrieve information, events or ideas from texts and use quotation and reference to text; to deduce, infer or interpret information, events or ideas from texts.
> **What you need:** Copies of *The Highwayman*, photocopiable page 32.
> **Cross-curricular link:** PSHE.

What to do

● Ask the children to think about how *The Highwayman* made them feel.

● Hand out individual copies of photocopiable page 32. Explain to the children that they need to think about how they felt at different points in the story, and note down the happiest, saddest, scariest and nastiest moment along the way.

● Encourage the children to really think about all their options for each answer. Stress that while the ghost story end might initially be thought to be the scariest, the moment when the redcoats tie Bess up with a gun is infinitely more frightening. Challenge them to think whether the happiest moment is the end or the beginning. Is the nastiest moment Tim overhearing Bess and the highwayman or one of the scenes with the soldiers? Or perhaps it's the implication that the landlord stands by and lets his daughter be mistreated?

Along the way

● How did *The Highwayman* make you feel? Note here the parts of the poem that you found:

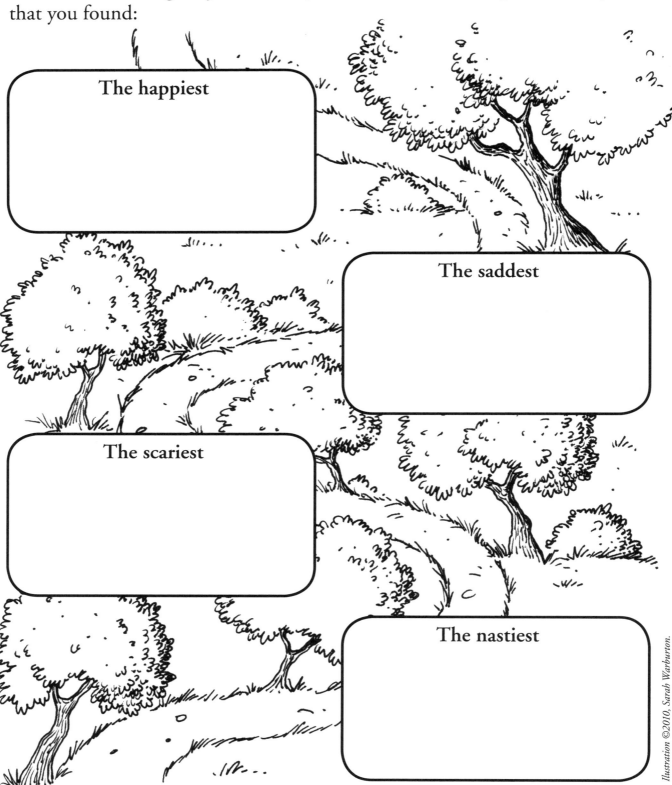

The happiest

The saddest

The scariest

The nastiest

Illustration ©2010, Sarah Warburton.